FUZZY DINOSAURS
& PREHISTORIC CREATURES

Lincoln
Children's Books

Brimming with creative inspiration, how-to projects, and useful information to enrich your everyday life, Quarto Knows is a favourite destination for those pursuing their interests and passions. Visit our site and dig deeper with our books into your area of interest: Quarto Creates, Quarto Cooks, Quarto Homes, Quarto Lives, Quarto Drives, Quarto Explores, Quarto Gifts, or Quarto Kids.

First Published in 2018 by Lincoln Children's Books,
an imprint of The Quarto Group.
The Old Brewery, 6 Blundell Street, London N7 9BH, United Kingdom.
T (0)20 7700 6700 F (0)20 7700 8066 **www.QuartoKnows.com**

Published in association with the Natural History Museum, London.

A catalogue record for this book is available from the British Library.

ISBN 978-1-78603-164-8

The illustrations were created in watercolour and edited digitally.
Set in Futura and LiviFont2017.

Published by Rachel Williams and Jenny Broom
Designed by Karissa Santos
Edited by Katy Flint
Production by Laura Grandi

Manufactured in Shenzhen, China HH022018

9 8 7 6 5 4 3 2 1

How To Use This Book

There are **seven** colouring charts in this book.

Each prehistoric creature on the colouring chart has a number.

Batrachognathus ②

How to say:
BAT-rag-O-NATH-us
Length: 0.7 metres
Survival skills:
Crunching dragonflies with its spear-shaped teeth.

Match each number to the Fact File on the opposite page.

You can get ideas for which colours to use from the pictures in the Fact Files – but no-one really knows what colours dinosaurs were. How will you choose to colour them in?

The Prehistoric World

Dinosaurs dominated the landscape for millions of years, but there were many other prehistoric creatures that lived alongside them.

Collected together in this book are creatures of the prehistoric sea, land and sky. They have been organised into charts for you to colour in and learn about. Look out for...

1. A **plant-eating** *Triceratops*, searching for palm leaves and avoiding *Tyrannosaurus rex*.

2. One of the **smallest** dinosaurs around, the turkey-sized *Compsognathus*.

3. A *Plesiosaurus* swimming slowly in the **sea** amongst dozens of ammonites.

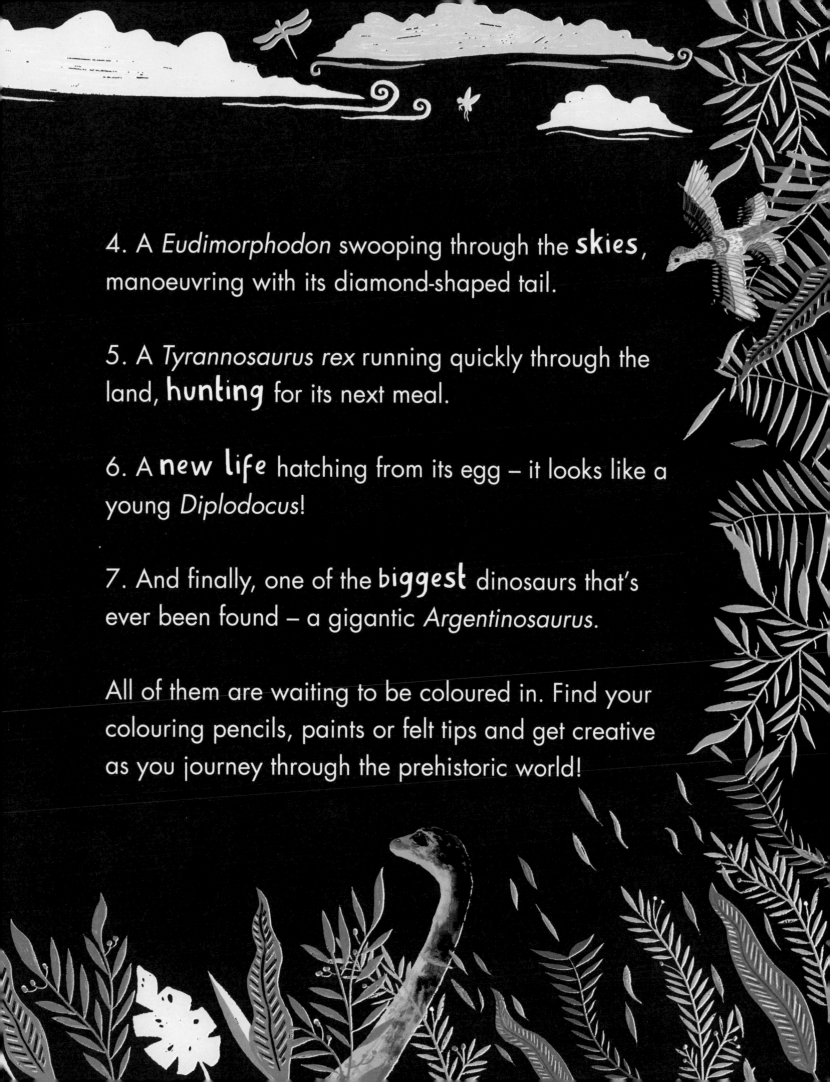

4. A *Eudimorphodon* swooping through the **skies**, manoeuvring with its diamond-shaped tail.

5. A *Tyrannosaurus rex* running quickly through the land, **hunting** for its next meal.

6. A **new life** hatching from its egg – it looks like a young *Diplodocus*!

7. And finally, one of the **biggest** dinosaurs that's ever been found – a gigantic *Argentinosaurus*.

All of them are waiting to be coloured in. Find your colouring pencils, paints or felt tips and get creative as you journey through the prehistoric world!

The Plant Eaters
Colour in these herbivores!

1 Stegosaurus

How to say: STEG-oh-SORE-us
Length: 9 metres
Survival skill: Swinging its tail spikes to ward off predators.

2 Diplodocus

How to say: DIP-low-DOCK-us
Length: 26 metres
Survival skill: Reaching leaves from tall trees with its long neck.

Gargoyleosaurus **3**

How to say:
gar-GOY-le-o-SAWR-us
Length: 4 metres
Survival skill: Having spiked armour on each side of its body for protection.

Triceratops **4**

How to say: try-SERRA-tops
Length: 9 metres
Survival skill: Fighting other *Triceratops* with its horns and head shield.

The Smallest

Colour in these tiny dinosaurs!

1. Fruitadens

How to say:
FROO-ta-denz
Length: 0.6 metres
Survival skill: Running speedily through the legs of larger dinosaurs.

2. Microraptor

How to say:
MIKE-row-rap-tor
Length: 0.8 metres
Survival skill: Gliding from tree to tree to escape predators or find prey.

3. Saltopus

How to say: sal-TO-pus
Length: Up to 1 metre
Survival skill: Running quickly and scavenging for food.

4. Lesothosaurus

How to say:
le-SO-toe-sore-us
Length: 1 metre
Survival skill:
Scanning for danger and outmanoeuvring predators.

5. Compsognathus

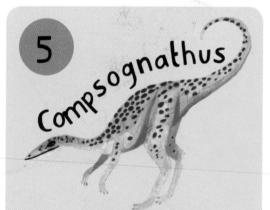

How to say:
komp-sog-NATH-us
Length: 1 metre
Survival skill:
Snatching prey with its three-fingered hands.

6. Wannanosaurus

How to say:
wah-NAN-oh-SORE-us
Length: 0.6 metres
Survival skill: Ramming rivals with its thick skull.

Sea Dwellers
Colour in these prehistoric swimmers!

1 Platypterygius

How to say:
plat-ee-teh-ree-GEE-us
Length: 7 metres
Survival skill:
Swimming with its streamlined and powerful body.

2 Pistosaurus

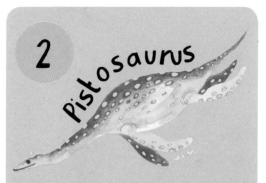

How to say:
PIS-toe-SORE-rus
Length: 3 metres
Survival skill:
Using its paddle-like flippers to push through water.

3 Malawania

How to say:
mal-a-wan-EE-a
Length: 3 metres
Survival skill:
Using its long snout to catch fish.

Plesiosaurus 4

How to say:
ple-SEE-o-SORE-us
Length: 3.5 metres
Survival skill: Preying on squid with its long, sharp teeth.

5 Archelon

How to say: ark-EH-lon
Length: 4 metres
Survival skill: Using its thick shell for protection.

High Fliers

Colour in these flying reptiles!

Archaeopteryx

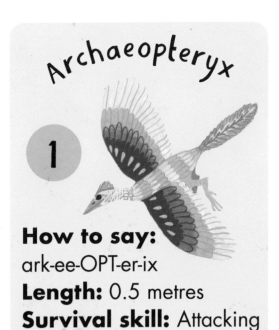

1

How to say:
ark-ee-OPT-er-ix
Length: 0.5 metres
Survival skill: Attacking prey with its jaws and clawed wings.

Batrachognathus

2

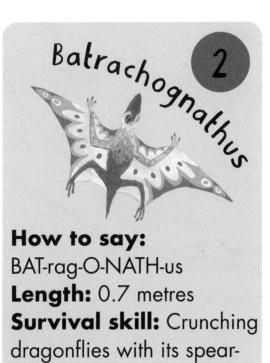

How to say:
BAT-rag-O-NATH-us
Length: 0.7 metres
Survival skill: Crunching dragonflies with its spear-shaped teeth.

Pterodactylus

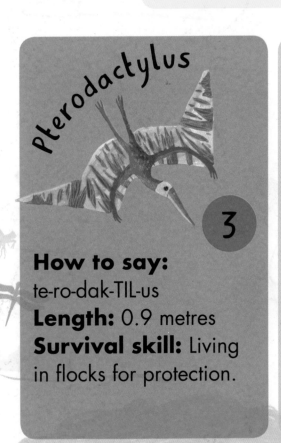

3

How to say:
te-ro-dak-TIL-us
Length: 0.9 metres
Survival skill: Living in flocks for protection.

Kuehneosaurus

4

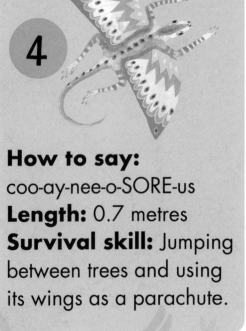

How to say:
coo-ay-nee-o-SORE-us
Length: 0.7 metres
Survival skill: Jumping between trees and using its wings as a parachute.

Eudimorphodon

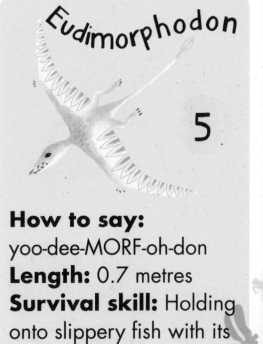

5

How to say:
yoo-dee-MORF-oh-don
Length: 0.7 metres
Survival skill: Holding onto slippery fish with its sharp teeth.

The Hunters

Colour in these predators!

1 — Giganotosaurus

How to say: gig-an-OH-toe-SORE-us
Length: 13 metres
Survival skill: Stealing other hunters' prey – as well as catching its own.

2 — Spinosaurus

How to say: SPINE-no-SORE-us
Length: 13–18 metres
Survival skill: Hunting in water for marine creatures with its crocodile-like snout.

3 — Velociraptor

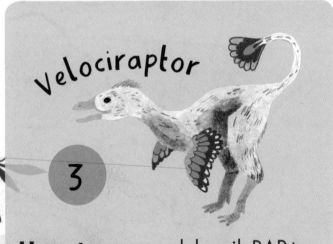

How to say: veh-loss-ih-RAP-tor
Length: 1.8 metres
Survival skill: Scientists think velociraptors worked in a pack to catch prey.

4 — Tyrannosaurus rex

How to say: tie-RAN-oh-SORE-us rex
Length: 12 metres
Survival skill: Catching prey and scaring scavengers with its power and ferocity.

New Life

Colour in these dinosaur babies!

Triceratops

1

How to say:
tri-SERRA-tops

Diplodocus

2

How to say:
DIP-low-DOCK-us

Tyrannosaurus rex

3

How to say:
tie-RAN-oh-SORE-us rex

Stegosaurus

4

How to say:
STEG-oh-SORE-us

The Biggest

Colour in this prehistoric giant, one of the largest dinosaurs of all time!

1

Argentinosaurus

How to say: AR-gent-eeno-sore-us
Length: 35 metres
Survival skill: Its incredible size protected it from any predators.

Learn More!

The Plant Eaters

Many plant-eating dinosaurs – called herbivores – lived in herds to protect them from hunters. Some are thought to have fed, nested and travelled together.

The Smallest

Small dinosaurs were easy prey for larger creatures. However, most ran on two legs and could hide in order to avoid being a larger dinosaur's dinner.

Sea Dwellers

While dinosaurs walked on land, the prehistoric seas teemed with life. Creatures such as fish, ammonites, marine reptiles and squid all lived in the ocean.

High Fliers

Flying reptiles and bird-like dinosaurs ruled the prehistoric skies. They had very light skeletons which meant they could fly. Many could take off from the ground, but some had to glide from high perches.

The Hunters

While some dinosaurs scavenged for dead meat, others hunted for prey. Many of these predators had sharp claws and serrated teeth, and their power and speed helped them to catch and kill other creatures.

New Life

Scientists think dinosaurs hatched from eggs, like reptiles and birds do today. Some dinosaurs looked after their eggs and young. We can tell this by how they arranged their nests.

The Biggest

Some dinosaurs grew to be extremely large, like the sauropods. Scientists are not yet sure how this group of dinosaurs grew to be so enormous. Being large meant that they were less likely to be attacked or eaten.

Dinosaur Timeline

Kuehneosaurus

Saltopus

250 – 200 million years ago

200 – 145 million

TRIASSIC	JURASSIC
Mid	Late	Early - Mid

Pistosaurus

Plesiosaurus

The dinosaurs and other prehistoric creatures lived in three different time periods. Look at the timeline below to see which prehistoric creatures lived when.

Pterodactylus

Microraptor

Diplodocus

T-rex

years ago

145 – 65 million years ago

CRETACEOUS

Late

Early

Late

Platypterygius

Also available in the series

Fuzzy Animals
by Papio Press

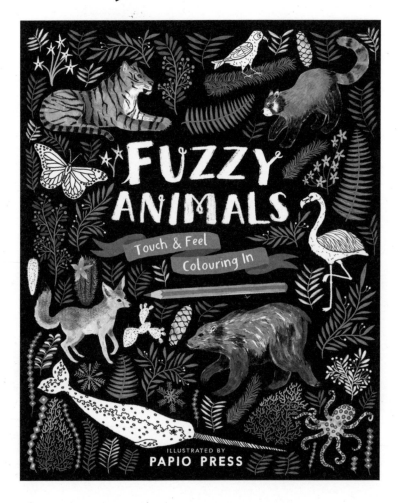

ISBN 978-1-78603-162-4

Explore seven habitats as you colour in each flocked animal chart. Meet tigers in the jungle, hammerhead sharks in the ocean and red pandas in the mountains. Featuring art of the world's best-loved and most spectacular animals to colour in. With facts for every creature to read and learn about.